# THE MODERN MIND
## AND
# THE VIRGIN BIRTH

BY

G. W. McPHERSON

*This book is dedicated to the deity of Our Lord and Saviour Jesus Christ and the inspiration of the Bible.*



YONKERS BOOK COMPANY
34 SAINT ANDREWS PLACE
YONKERS, NEW YORK

*Printed in the United States of America*
Published July, 1923.

## FOREWORD

This volume comprises a brief compendium of facts regarding the Virgin Birth of Christ and presents the current objections to this basic Christian doctrine with answers thereto. The discussion, it is hoped, will prove valuable to the average person who is too busy to make a thorough investigation of the doctrines of Christianity and to the scholar as well. Many skeptical minds have voiced opposition to the incarnation and deity of Christ. There are also students in our institutions of learning who have been led to question the Virgin Birth. The author has endeavored to get at the heart of the problem, and make clear that all classes of intelligent persons can accept, without mental reservation, and with a strong, glowing faith the fact of our Lord's supernatural human origin. The query of all queries still is, "What shall I do then with Jesus which is called Christ?" May the reader be helped by this message to answer for himself this momentous question.

THE AUTHOR.

## CONTENTS

# The Modern Mind and The Virgin Birth

## CHAPTER I

### A GENERAL APPROACH

This message, as the title may suggest, will consist of an examination of current objections to the Virgin Birth of our Lord Jesus Christ.

The terms Virgin Birth and Incarnation, though they may be interpreted differently, will be used interchangeably, for it is difficult to see how either one can be intelligently employed in a discussion concerning our Lord's human origin, apart from the other.

It is hoped that the present chapter will serve to prepare for what will follow, by calling attention to the divergent views of those who accept and those who reject, as fact, the Virgin Birth, and to the increasing religious unrest that is everywhere in evidence today.

## Immaculate Conception

In order to remove confusion in the thought of some, a discrimination should be made between the Virgin Birth and the Immaculate Conception. The latter has reference to the Virgin Mary and may be viewed as a speculative dogma that was established centuries after our Lord was born. This dogma is an hypothesis, i.e., an assumption regarding the nature of the Virgin for which there is found no basis in Holy Scripture. The dogma affirms that the Virgin was absolutely sinless, that by a special work of God in her nature, she was conceived without sin, made free from every moral imperfection and tendency to evil, and thus was prepared to become the mother of our Lord.

Prior to its acceptance there was much opposition to this dogma in the early Church. Augustine and others of note opposed the idea that Mary was free from original sin, and the Protestant Communions, including the Reformers, never accepted it as a Scripture doctrine, or as necessary to the sinlessness of our Lord. They have always believed that our Lord's perfection as man, or his sinlessness and triumph over evil was the result of his Incarnation and not of an immaculate conception in the pre-natal life of his noble mother. If it is true that the secret of His sinlessness is found in a perfect humanity which He inherited, would it not follow that temptation would have been impossible to Him, and that His ideal life as an example to His disciples could not in any sense have been the result of a moral effort and triumph over evil on His part? Furthermore, is not such a view calculated to reduce the example of our Lord to that bordering on mockery? From the New Testament it is obvious that our Lord was a real human being, tempted by Satan as men are always tempted, and that the battle he fought against temptation was a real and not a sham battle. The following Scriptures will make clear, without further comment, that the Protestant contention regarding the mother of our Lord is unanswerable, and in the light of which it is unscriptural to refer to the Virgin Mary as, "the mother of God."

"For verily he took not on him the

nature of angels; but he took on him the seed of Abraham.

"Wherefore in all things it behoved him to be made like unto his brethren, that he might be a merciful and faithful high priest in things pertaining to God, to make reconciliation for the sins of the people.

"For in that he himself hath suffered being tempted, he is able to succor them that are tempted."—Heb. 2:16-18.

"For we have not an high priest which cannot be touched with the feeling of our infirmities; but was in all points tempted like as we are, yet without sin."—Heb. 4:15.

### The Virgin Birth

By the Virgin Birth is meant, as the Gospels of Matthew and Luke reveal, that our Lord did not have a human father, but was begotten of the Holy Spirit and born of a Virgin; consequently he was a new type of man, the head of a new race of spiritual beings as Adam was the head of a new race of human beings.

Matthew states the Incarnation in these words: "Now the birth of Jesus Christ was on this wise: When as his mother

Mary was espoused (as we say today "engaged") to Joseph, before they came together, she was found with child of the Holy Spirit."—Matt. 1:18.

In Luke the Incarnation is set forth in the words of the angel to Mary: "The Holy Spirit shall come upon thee, and the power of the Highest shall overshadow thee; therefore also that holy One that shall be born of thee shall be called the Son of God."—Luke, 1:35.

This then is the basic doctrine that has always been believed by the Christian people, from the Apostles down to the present, but that is denied today by a certain class of scholars, some of whom call themselves scientists and religious liberalists, and are teachers in educational institutions and preachers, here and there, in Christian pulpits.

### Investigation

If it is true, as few will deny, that there appears to be a growing skepticism regarding the Virgin Birth of our Lord Jesus Christ, then the hour has arrived when the rank and file of the Christian people should become informed as to the basis for belief in this doctrine. Silence and indifference in a time like this are calculated to misrepresent and do much harm to the future of Christianity. The cause and honor of our Lord demand, therefore, that some pertinent questions should be asked and answered. Thoughtful men everywhere, in pulpit and pew, should face the present religious unrest and pronounce to the world in no uncertain fashion their reasons for faith in this doctrine. Would it not be helpful to the Master's cause to discuss some such questions as the following?

1. Is there something concerning this basic doctrine to which intelligent minds may reasonably object, and if so what is it?

2. What is the real problem in regard to the Virgin Birth of our Lord, and is it to be found in this doctrine or in those who reject it?

3. Can educated people, in a day of advancing knowledge, scientific progress and searching literary criticism, accept, as fact, the Virgin Birth?

It is believed that the objections to this doctrine, as found in infidel and rationalistic literature, are not the result of new knowledge but are characteristic of those who are dominated by a naturalistic philosophy of the universe and who lack moral comprehension of great spiritual reality; that only those who have lost the spirit of Christ, or who have never had the sense of the presence and power of God in their lives object to the Virgin Birth. This form of unbelief seems to be characteristic of many persons today, and may be viewed as an illustration of the subtle dangers of naturalism in religion, or of the age-long problem which is always inherent in the nature of a certain class of men—their indisposition to believe in an Almighty God as Creator.

### Contention of Modernists

There are those who insist that thoughtful men can no longer hold to the faith of our fathers and that Christianity must be restated in new terms that are in harmony with modern science and acceptable to "modern men," even though it be at the cost of the rejection of those old cherished Bible doctrines which, for nineteen hundred years, the Christian people have believed and loved, which doctrines, they say, we must cast aside, as we would a worn-out garment, and accept in their place the vague, indefinite and everchanging postulates and conclusions of science and philosophy.

Rationalists generally affirm that "modern men" have a new conception of God and the universe which forbids belief in miracles, and which compels them to abandon the age-long faith in a personal Deity. God, to them, is, in reality, not personal, though they use our Christian terms and address Him as Father, but, rather, an abstract philosophic conception of a universal Energy, or Principle, which can be interpreted only in the light of evolution, and by men of science; consequently they argue for the necessity of a new and everchanging theology which, they affirm, must be built to harmonize with the new and everchanging and enlarging conception of God, the universe, and advancing scientific knowledge. Since, they say, the miracles, including the Virgin Birth, cannot be made to fit into this new conception of God and the universe, belief in them must be abandoned. They tell us that to believe in the Virgin Birth implies a rejection of scientific truth, that this doctrine runs counter to natural law, and we should bravely face the facts, welcome the new light of science, take what is sound out of the wreckage of the old beliefs, and with the new views seek to win "modern men" to a new faith in a new universe, a new Christ, a new Bible and a new conception of God. This statement is not exaggerated or overdrawn as the more candid of the modernists themselves will admit. If the Christian world will not accept them as the true leaders and prophets of "the new age," they declare that the masses will, and that the "thinking people" will forsake the churches leaving them to wither up and perish from what they term "the dry rot of a dead theology."

On the other hand there are those who represent Evangelical Christianity and who affirm that the biblical revelation of a personal God as Creator constitutes the only true conception, and that the Bible in all its teachings is in harmony with exact science.

Mr. James T. Bowron of Birmingham,

Alabama, a thoughtful and able layman, who made a valuable review of the manuscript for this book, portions of which are incorporated in the text, said among other comments, part of which will be quoted later:

"Mankind must be divided into two classes, those who do believe and those who do not believe in a personal Deity who was a Creator. Those who do not believe in a personal Deity and Creator may be, and are asked, *en passant,* If you do not believe in a personal God as Creator, how did this world come to exist as it is today? Such agnostics are precluded from claiming that the world has always been as it is today, because every scientist, without exception, will agree that geology shows us the earth as it exists represents a sequence of changes, with materially differential conditions existing from one epoch to another, during which animal life, and especially the more complicated and delicate human life, could not have existed. With our knowledge of erosion and sedimentary deposition and of atmospheric conditions during the carboniferous period, we can say definitely that man could not have lived upon the earth until the post-glacial period was ended, which is a period comparatively recent and by no means far removed from the records of antiquity open to the archaeologists in Egypt and Assyria. Every school boy learns the axiom "*Ex nihilo nihil fit.*" When the world was without form and void, before it had passed through the sequences which are read by geologists as from a book, there must have been some force to produce and develop the extremely complicated process of animal and vegetable life which now exists. It may suffice to ask the nonbeliever in God as Creator to find some method of accounting for this creation and development and leave him to solve the problem while we pass on to the other class of men, namely, those who do believe in God as a Creator."

This then is the situation we are compelled, as lovers of God and his truth, to face today, and to examine with the most painstaking care and see if what the modernists are telling is true as to both science and Revelation. Remember that this whole question of a personal God and of Creation has a direct bearing upon the Virgin Birth of our Lord, because it brings us face to face with the question of the integrity and authority of the Scriptures. The Scriptures clearly teach that our Lord was born miraculously. The modernists say that the story of our Lord's human origin is a myth. Surely, if the Virgin Birth is only a myth we should know it; if it is true we should know it. The churches are called to study for themselves the objections to this great doctrine and see whether the new views of modernists are worthy of acceptance. If, e.g., it is evident that what they say regarding the origin and history of man and of the Virgin Birth and Deity of our Lord is not supported by facts it is only reasonable to believe that they are in error in regard to that which they claim to be the true basis for a new Christian faith.

### Incarnation and Science

The Christian world is compelled today to face this old, yet new, perennial problem as, perhaps, never before, and ask: Is it true that the Virgin Birth of our

Lord is in conflict with science and therefore cannot be believed by "modern men" who are in sympathy with new knowledge?

The position taken in this discussion is, that "modern men," all classes of intelligent persons can accept this doctrine of Christianity, without mental reservation, and with a strong, glowing faith, that the Virgin Birth is not in conflict with science, and that the religious problems which perplex men should be dealt with frankly and fully. It hardly needs be stated that Christianity is not the enemy of science, for between God's two great books—the Bible and Nature—there is no conflict. To quote Sir Robert Anderson: "Never until our own times have Scripture and science been (so far) in accord, but the changes that have harmonized them have been in science and not in Scripture." We should eagerly assimilate the results of true science. The laboratory need not be the enemy of God and his truth. Science has made all men her debtors. The results of science have tended to confirm rather than disprove the Bible, as modern archaeology and geology abundantly bear witness. Professor Dana, the eminent geologist, declared that, "the first chapter of Genesis and science are in accord."

It is well to remember that many noted scientists have affirmed their belief in the Incarnation. Even so great a scientist as Huxley—the agnostic—while rejecting the Virgin Birth on other grounds, said that on scientific grounds he had no objection to it.

The Rev. J. Wilson Sutton, D.D., of New York has recently, by request of his congregation, published a sermon which he preached in Trinity Chapel, entitled: "Birth From A Virgin," and in which he has given facts of much value. We take the liberty to quote him:

"Those who would have us give up the Virgin Birth on scientific grounds only succeed in leading us into a serious scientific difficulty. Since the beginning of the world, millions upon millions of children have been born of human mothers through the agency of human fathers, and never has it been known that the union of human father and human mother brought into the world other than a human person. But Jesus Christ is a Divine Person and to claim that He came into the world in the way that human persons come into it is to take a thoroughly unscientific position . . . . Our Lord has a human mother because He has a human nature; He has a Divine Father because He is a Divine Person. His human nature was brought into being and united with His Divine Person through the operation of the Holy Spirit because, while a human father in union with a human mother could have produced a human nature, and have brought into the world a human person, *a human father in union with a human mother could not possibly have brought into the world a Divine Person, or united a human nature with a Divine Person, except by running absolutely counter to the natural law of which people make so much. I am not prepared to say that God could not have brought His Divine Son into the world through the agency of St. Joseph and St. Mary. I am prepared to say that if He had done so He would have violated the recognized and universally scientific law that the union of human father and human mother brings into the world a human person, and that in so far this law would have been discredited.''*

But it is the boast of modernists that this great doctrine is in conflict with science. They say, ''When science proves it we will believe it.'' What childish nonsense! Science, while it has made a great contribution to man's comfort, health and knowledge, can prove but little in the realm of the supernatural. And we are now dealing with a supernatural event in human history. Science can help us to a more perfect understanding of the laws of nature and its phenomena, but there is a line beyond which science cannot pass. In dealing with religion the theologian can well afford to say to the scientist, hands off. Theology, which is the science of God, science cannot construct. Even in the realm of natural phenomena science has made slow progress and cannot explain many of the most common yet age-long problems. Take, e.g., the problem of sleep. Have scientists explained sleep? Of course they do not refuse to sleep because its mystery has baffled them. They resign themselves once in every twenty-four hours to this good old doctor, and out of every fifty years they are unconscious about sixteen years. Of course scientists do not refuse to eat because they cannot fully explain how food is translated into blood and bone and muscle and nerves and brain cells. Have they faith in the dining-room and not in the Church and the Word of God? Do they deny the fact of gravitation because they do not understand gravitation? Do they hide themselves from the sun's rays because they are yet unable to analyze all the actual and potential elements and powers of light and heat? If science proceeds on the assumption that all phenomena in nature are the result of natural causes, why should the Christian people be viewed as "unscientific," because they ascribe a supernatural cause to the presence in history of a supernatural person? Some day men may be able to understand all the secrets of nature. Most scientists believe this. The Christian Revelation affirms that some day "we shall know even as also we are known," and this includes knowledge of all natural and spiritual phenomena, including the Virgin

Birth. It is not stating it too strongly to affirm that, in the light of all the facts connected with our Lord's life and teaching, it is unscientific to deny or reject, as an article of faith, the Virgin Birth, and that such a denial, or even a neutral attitude toward it, is calculated to challenge, not alone the testimony of Scripture but also any reasonable hypothesis, and to stultify our highest intelligence. Moreover, if those who assume this attitude are scientists or Christians then reasonable men must be at a loss to understand how they can be either.

### Incarnation and Reason

In the realm of cold logic, the facts, when understood, will argue for acceptance of the Virgin Birth of our Lord. Is there a sane, rational person who claims that he can account for the remarkable personality, teachings and miracles of our Lord and yet deny his Incarnation? Let the religious liberalists, who are vocal in their eulogies of science, explain Jesus Christ. We challenge them to the task, and we welcome their explanation. They will indulge in evasions or denials but they will not attempt the impossible without giving to men a bisected, distorted, fragmentary, mutilated Christ —a counterfeit and not the real Christ of the Gospels. It is easy for unreasoning minds to deny the Virgin Birth, to pull down and destroy, but have they an explanation of our Lord Jesus Christ? There is a radicalism in religion as unsound and untrue as the radicalism in Russian Socialism, but it is only the fatigue of a formal religion when men have not had the experience of Christ in their lives, or the moral stamina to keep it up. Their theories are not based on sound reasoning or Scriptures; they are merely the froth and foam of their fancy; they have no foundation in fact; they cannot stand the light of investigation and truth; they perish in the light of day. But notwithstanding the irrationality of Modernism, many uninformed persons who cannot think for themselves and weigh evidence have been deceived and led astray from the Christian faith by persistent misrepresentations of the truth. Those who believe the Virgin Birth, therefore, and others are called upon to make a fresh study of this ancient Christian doctrine. The Church can well afford to welcome investigation of her time-honored faith, the foundations of which are immovable. We have no fear of a searching criticism of the truth, for honest criticism will only strengthen faith, awaken hope and intensify love by making clear the great significance of the Virgin Birth of our Lord. This fact will be seen more clearly in its relation to the life and teachings of our Lord, as the fulfilment of ancient prophecy, as that momentous event in which we see a new disclosure of God's great plan of making known his love and salvation for men. Thus will the Incarnation shine forth with fresh significance and in a new and radiant splendor.

### Incarnation and Faith

Much of the difficulty with those who deny the miraculous conception of our Lord is due to an inadequate or false idea of the proper function or fundamental place of faith in man's life. The rationalists underestimate faith, yet they unconsciously assert it and continuously act upon it. Men live from day to day because they yield their life to that which they do not understand. What the Apostle Paul declared, in reference to the secret of a continuous Christian life, when he said, "We walk by faith," applies also to all men. All human action, as all experience in the divine life, is conditioned on faith. Why should men object to the proper function of faith in their attitude to God and to his method of making himself known? Here is found an illustration of the unreason of reason, or the irrationality of those who reject the Virgin Birth. Has not our Lord ever baffled explanation on natural grounds? But has faith no function to perform, no part to play here in a reasonable study, or correct understanding of Jesus Christ? Surely this applies with force and unanswerable logic to the Scripture account of the human origin of our Lord. It is unscientific, unreasonable and in conflict with true faith to deny the Incarnation. By accepting this doctrine time and experience will demonstrate the wisdom of faith.

**Incarnation and Miracles**

One of the common objections to the Virgin Birth is that miracles do not happen. Doubtless from God's standpoint there are no miracles, but from man's point of view there are events in human history which are properly viewed as miraculous. God does not violate his own laws, but he can bring into play a new law or a law regarding which men are totally ignorant. It is a miracle to men; it is natural to God. "For, how many years," says Mr. Bowron, "after we transmitted our telegraphic messages along a wire, elapsed without our discovering that we could send the messages without the wire? For how many years have we believed that none could see into the inside of a box, or a man's pocketbook folded up in his pocket, or into his stomach, and yet, today, with the *X*-ray we have not the least difficulty in obtaining these results which would have appeared as miracles to previous generations, but only because we know more of God's laws which have always been in existence, but simply we did not know them until now.

No one can explain by what law, or by what suspension of law by God, the centripetal force is suspended when a comet is at its perihelion and about to be burned up, and, on the contrary, the centrifugal force is suspended when the comet is at its aphelion and in danger of being attacked by the superior gravitation forces of some other solar or stellar system. Scientists above all men who know these wonderful things to be true should be the very last to cavil at recorded demonstrations of God's power."

To affirm that miracles do not happen, or that God cannot work above man's reason, or beyond man's comprehension of phenomena, is to postulate a false view of man and to place God in a sorry plight indeed. It is to assume that men are fully competent to determine what God can or cannot do, how he works or must not work, and that men know all about natural law. All this is involved in a denial of miracles. And is not such an assumption both irrational and foolish? Is it not a greater assumption than to believe that God is not a slave in his universe, and that, to suit his own purpose, he can, if needs be, in order to reveal his power and love, change a machine which he himself has made? If this is the proper conception of God and of his world, and if he has created his universe in any such mechanical fashion, it follows that he cannot work a miracle in it, "and there is no point in our arguing in defense of the Virgin Birth of Christ."

Those who argue against the Incarnation on the ground that miracles do not happen should be ready to explain what appears to be the greatest of all miracles, the origin of all life, of man, birds, beasts, fishes, etc. etc. Is not the beginning of human life, e.g., an unsolved mystery? Science cannot help us here. At best the only reasonable hypothesis or affirmation is to say, in the language of Scripture, "In the beginning God created." Has the evolutionist any other explanation to give? Evolution deals only with the development of life; it cannot be defined as creation. And what more can be affirmed regarding the problem of moral consciousness? Is not this also a miracle to men? As Tennyson well expressed it:

> "This main miracle that thou art thou."

Whatever our theory of development and moral consciousness, we cannot escape the fact of origin. "We know," as Mr. Bowron reminds us, "how life is transmitted, but we have absolutely no shadow of information as to how life in any department of nature began, except as we derive our knowledge from the Holy Scriptures, recognized by evangelical churches as the only infallible rule of faith and practice." As Mr. Bryan stated it to the writer: "The Virgin Birth of Christ is no more a mystery than my birth, only it is different." "In the beginning" God must have created a body or those potentialities of life which developed rapidly into a body. But could not the Creator produce a new and distinct type of body for the special manifestation of himself to men, as the Scriptures reveal he did do in the person of our Lord? "Wherefore when he cometh into the world, he saith, . . . but a body hast thou prepared me."—Heb. 10:5.

To quote Mr. Bowron again: "The belief that the Infinite God planned and created the universe in whole involves the power to create in part. If any believer in God as Creator believes in his power to have created the first man without that man having a mother, how can he limit the Creator's power and refuse to believe that it was quite as easy for God to create a body either alone or in *parturio* without a human father? Obviously there is no greater difficulty as to the recorded birth of Jesus Christ without a father than the recorded creation of Adam without a mother. . . . To the Scriptures alone we must look, as believers in a God as Creator, to see how he created and how he originated life, and we find it."

**Strange Silence**

Does it not appear strange, in the light of the well-known propaganda of the modernists, in printed page, in pulpit, pew, university and conventions, that Christian men, who believe the Bible to be a revelation of truth from God, remain so passive and silent? Do they fear to affirm their faith in the biblical doctrines of our holy religion? Can they imagine that this onslaught on vital Christian truth will blow over, spend itself and be forgotten, and to ignore it and those who are undermining the foundation of the Church is the wisest method to pursue? Surely such an attitude is unworthy of reasonable men. There are those who seem to believe that the wisest procedure is to preach Christ and him crucified and risen and ignore the arguments which the modernists employ in their attack upon the inspiration of the Bible and the deity of our Lord. But how can Christ and him crucified be intelligently preached today without also meeting the arguments of those who are denying the inspiration and authority of the Book? "If the foundations be destroyed, what can the righteous do?"—Ps. 11:3. In every church there are men and women who are greatly confused because they have learned the point of view of those who deny the integrity of the Bible and teach that the individual consciousness is the basis of authority in Christianity. Surely, the churches must stoutly refute this heresy or become a party to the work of the boldest religious embezzlers of the ages. If the churches continue to ignore it, or fail to meet the problem they may as well have no constitution. Yet timid Christians, in pulpit and pew, remain silent while witnessing the subtle destruction of the Gospel. "Do they want our children to deny the redemption of the cross, and our students taught this rationalism and filling our pulpits and controlling our churches? Men can remain in many of the chief pulpits of the land and deny the holy nativity of our Lord and the churches are becoming Unitarian while we sleep."

### The Great Fundamentals

It should be remembered that it is against the integrity and inspiration of the Bible that Modernism is making its attack by substituting man's authority in place of the Sacred Word. Rev. Dr. William P. Merril, pastor of the Brick Presbyterian Church, New York, is quoted by the press as having said in a recent sermon that, "those will win in the modern religious problem who reveal most of the Christ spirit." That sounds like the words of Canon Barnes of London, spoken before the British Association of Scientists in 1921—"To the Christian who accepts modern biological principles the Christ spirit is the supreme and final power in the evolution of man,'' by which the Canon meant that modern biological principles, or man's scientific conceptions, are the basis of authority in religion and that to this type of man the Christ spirit becomes a power in spiritual evolution. It is to the modernist a matter of small moment to reject the Virgin Birth of Christ and his teachings, and the interpretation of Christ as given by his Apostles—in short to reject the Bible as authority—but it is a matter of the utmost gravity to reject what the modernist calls ''the Christ spirit.'' Here then is found a concise statement of the deceptive phraseology and teaching of Modernism, and it furnishes likewise a striking illustration of inconsistency in dealing with the truth concerning Jesus Christ. ''If ye love me ye will keep my commandments,'' are our Lord's words, and we must test the spirit of men by their attitude to Jesus Christ, who said that his words are the final authority. ''Heaven and earth shall pass away, but my words shall not pass away.''

This misleading phrase, ''the Christ spirit,'' which is the last refuge of a refined and subtle unbelief, is much employed today by the spiritist, evolutionist and modernist—by all those, in fact, who reject the inspiration and divine authority of the Bible. But how can men consistently exalt or emulate the spirit of our Lord and deny the supernatural Christ of the Gospels? They say, "emulate the spirit of Christ," while at the same time they reject the fundamental teachings of Christ regarding himself, and the authority and inspiration of the Bible which our Lord endorsed, calling the latter "dictation." To them "the Bible is only the product of men expressing their human conceptions of God under the natural providences of God and therefore constitute but man's growth in the conception of God." They say "the Bible is full of errors that can only be reviewed by the modern scientific mind and rejected at will." The purpose of those who reject the Virgin Birth and authority of Christ, therefore, is to break down the authority of the Bible as the inspired word of God and the Church as a divine institution and get control of the churches. But it should not be forgotten that,

*"Christ the Living Word and the Bible the Written Word must stand or fall together. These are the two great fundamentals of the Christian faith which find expression at the Lord's table where believers proclaim the deity of Christ, his atoning sacrifice and personal return. Here is the core of Fundamentalism. These are the great fundamentals which make a fool of Modernism and its monkey theology."*

This discussion is concluded with a further quotation from Mr. Bowron's able comments on the contents of this chapter:

"The Scriptures themselves are supported in their accuracy by their unity and agreement although written over 1800 years—in different countries, in three different languages, by men ranging from crowned kings to herdsmen and fishermen, men who were highly learned and men who were quite unlearned—and yet all agreeing in every cardinal point of doctrine and giving furthermore information of an historical, personal, geographical and astronomical nature, which when first read was not understood but which has been confirmed after the invention of the telescope, the discovery by archaeologists of ruins covered up, and inscriptions, letters and documents which had been forgotten for thousands of years. Their supernatural origin is confirmed by the character of the doctrines taught both in the Old and New Testaments, differentiating, especially in the latter from the teachings proceeding from natural men. Finally, the supernatural character and value of the collection of books under that name is vouched for by its marvelous and unique preservation through the ages when all other books of similar antiquity have perished; further vouched for and mathematically demonstrated by the extraordinary fulfilments of prophecy, working out in many cases to the very month and day, bearing upon such events as the captivity and restoration of Israel, the coming of the Redeemer as to time and place and tribe, his rejection, sufferings, death and resurrection, the destruction of Jerusalem under the Romans, the subsequent defilement of the sanctuary by the Moslems, the termination of the temporal power of the Pope, the gradual removal of the Moslem power from the defilement of the sanctuary in Jerusalem, and the return of the Jews to the Holy Land. These predictions are so numerous and fulfilled with so much accuracy as to preclude any possibility of chance or coincidence, and the original prophecies have been preserved throughout the intervening centuries by the non-believers in Jesus Christ, the Jews, to whom were committed the oracles of God. To these Scriptures, and to them alone, we must look, therefore, as our authority. . . . They alone tell how God formed man out of the dust of the ground—and that is all man is today—largely water, with some organic matter, phosphorus and lime, a little sulphur, salt, etc. It does not require long for his frame to return to the dust from which it came. It does not say that God made man out of a plant, or out of an amoeba, or a jelly fish, or an amphibian, or a lizard, or a monkey, but he made man after His own likeness and He breathed into him the breath of life, which would not have been necessary if He had caused man to develop out of some other living form of animal life."

This lengthy quotation will serve to remind the reader of the fact that to the Bible and the Bible alone we must look for our authority as to creation, redemption and salvation, and when Modernism casts this authority aside, it is like a ship adrift upon a treacherous, raging sea, without chart and compass, whose mariners strive in the stress of the storm and the darkness of the night to get a glimpse of the North Star.

## CHAPTER II

### OBJECTION

**The story of Christ's birth, as related by Matthew and Luke, is an interpolation, i.e., something that was added to these Gospels centuries after they had been written.**

This is one of the common objections to the Virgin Birth which is frequently voiced today.

If the Christian world should become convinced that this proposition is established, as fact, doubtless some radical changes would result in Christianity. But when the truth is known, it will be seen how utterly baseless is this objection, for there is not found in any trustworthy literature, ancient or modern, the slightest warrant for this assumption.

The New Testament, as we have it today, is admitted by scholars of nearly every shade of opinion, to have been written before the close of the first century

A.D., and during this early period there is the most conclusive proof that the Christian people believed in the Virgin Birth of Christ. Moreover, the historic documents which serve as a basic for faith in the Virgin Birth have been verified as reliable parts of the earliest known manuscripts of the New Testament.

The Apostles Creed, in its earliest form, is known to have been in existence in the early part of the second century, so says Harnack, Zahn and Kattenbusch, and in this early form of the Creed are found these words: "Born of the Holy Spirit and the Virgin Mary."

Ignatius of Antioch, who is believed to have been a disciple of the Apostles, and who by some scholars is claimed to have lived from about 90 to 150 A.D., speaks of "the virginity of Mary and her child-bearing," Epistle to the Ephesians XIX.

This same authority also says: "Let no man be called good who mixes good with evil. For they speak of Christ not that they may preach Christ but that they may reject Christ. . . . They also calumniate his being born of a Virgin."—Letter to the Trallians Chap. VI.

Dr. Sutton's statement in the following paragraph, bearing on this matter, has for its basis facts that are generally known by biblical students. He says:

"The chapters in Matthew and Luke in which the record of the Virgin Birth appears, are found in all unmutilated manuscripts of the New Testament—there are many such manuscripts but from none are these chapters omitted—and they are found in all versions and translations of the manuscripts known to be genuine. There are but two versions in which they do not appear; one is known as the Gospel of the Ebionites, i.e., a version used by a sect in the early Church which denied the divinity of Christ and therefore could not admit that he was born in an unusual manner, the other was the Gospel of Luke, used by a man named Marcion, a strange person, who held that the God of the Old Testament was different from the God of the New Testament and taught that matter was essentially evil, and therefore could not consistently accept the doctrine of the Incarnation."—From, "Born of a Virgin."

A word of explanation should be added

to Dr. Sutton's reference to the Gospel of Luke which he says that Marcion, who denied the Incarnation, had in his possession. Marcion mutilated this Gospel, in the interest of his strange theories, by cutting out the story of the Virgin Birth.

From the above facts it is therefore evident that this objection contains not a shred of truth that can commend it to thoughtful minds.

## CHAPTER III

### OBJECTION

**The two stories of the Virgin Birth, as given by Matthew and Luke, including their genealogical records, are contradictory.**

Here also is another objection of which much has been said in recent years.

A careful study of the records in Matthew and Luke will convince any honest seeker after the truth as to their genuineness.

Matthew tells the story from Joseph's point of view and Luke tells it from Mary's point of view, and what one omits the other supplies, one being supplementary to the other.

As might well be expected, Luke goes more into detail than does Matthew, for Mary knew more about the sacred mystery than Joseph. Both, however, agree in the central fact in the story—that Jesus was born of a Virgin.

As Dr. Sutton well says in his sermon already referred to: "If we had only the account of Matthew we should be left in ignorance as to the perplexity of Mary, when it was revealed to her that she had been chosen to be the Lord's mother. If we had only the account of Luke we should know nothing of Joseph's anxiety when he discovered that his espoused wife was great with child. Thus the two records form a complete whole, and while written from different points of view are consistent in every detail."

Regarding the genealogies, it is true that they present problems but these are not insuperable, and cannot in anywise weaken the central fact that Jesus was born of a Virgin. These problems however have been cleared up. For a full discussion of this matter, the reader is referred to the books as listed below.*

---

*"The Virgin Birth: A Critical Examination"—by T. J. Thorbourn (Soc. for Promoting Christian Knowledge, London, or Macmillan Company, New York).

"Does It Make Any Difference? or the Virgin Birth of Christ"—by I. M. Haldeman, D. D. (Phila. School of the Bible).

"The Destructive Denial, or Jesus Not Joseph's

All great authorities agree that the genealogies were an original part of the Gospels and not a free invention of the Evangelists or of scribes at a later day, and that they contain no insuperable difficulties or apparent discrepancies that cannot be satisfactorily explained.

But our opponents say, "Is there not a contradiction in the genealogy in Luke 3:23?" Let us see. Here are Luke's words:

"And Jesus himself began to be about thirty years of age, being, as was supposed, the son of Joseph, which was the son of Heli."

The objection to this passage is, that while Matthew says that Joseph was the son of Jacob, Luke says that he was the son of Heli, and in what sense then could he be both of Jacob and Heli?

Dr. Scofield in commenting on this says:

"He could not be by natural generation the son of both Jacob and Heli. But

---

Son"—by Rev. R. E. Neighbor (Bible Truth Depot, Livenga, Pa.).

"The Virgin Birth of Christ"—by James Orr, D.D. (Scribner's Sons, New York).

in Luke it is not said that Heli begat Joseph, so that the natural explanation is that Joseph was the son-in-law of Heli, who was, like himself, a descendant of David. That in that case he should be called son of Heli, would be in accord with Jewish usage."—C. I. Scofield's Reference Bible, footnotes on Luke 3:23.

To what Jewish usage does Dr. Scofield refer, it may be asked? It was the custom of the Jews to trace the line of descent through the father who was the legal head of the household, or in some cases through the father-in-law, and this would naturally explain the apparent discrepancy in this case.

This usage may account for the name of Joseph being found in the record. Thus note Matthew's words: "and Jacob begat Joseph the husband of Mary, of whom was born Jesus, who is called Christ."—Matt. 1:16. It is clearly unfair exegesis to infer from these words, as has often been done by captious critics, that Matthew intended to convey the idea that Joseph was the human father of Jesus, for the context plainly shows that he meant nothing of the sort. He only stated that Joseph was the husband of Mary, but in verse eighteen he took pains to state that Joseph was her espoused husband. In this same verse he reveals that at this time Mary was with child by the Holy Spirit.

Dr. James Orr throws light on this: "Matthew introduces his genealogy for the very purpose of showing that Jesus had the legal rights of a son of Joseph. . . . The Evangelists are very careful in the language they use. Matthew has a periphrasis expressly to avoid this idea that Joseph was the human father of Jesus, 'Jacob begat Joseph the husband of Mary of whom was born Jesus, who is called Christ.' Luke carefully inserts the clause, 'being as was supposed the son of Joseph,' a clause found in all the texts." —"The Virgin Birth of Christ," page 101-102.

Thus it is seen that both Luke and Matthew were careful not to say that Jesus was the natural son of Joseph, and that the common objection "If Joseph were not the father of Jesus why was his name given in the genealogy as his father?", falls empty to the ground.

The above illustrates how the critic reads into the Bible what is not there, and how superficial or ignorant persons would accept his words without investigating for themselves—a lamentably common trait, that is characteristic of many of our present-day scholars and their misguided students.

In no true sense can any apparent discrepancy in these genealogical accounts prove their errancy. If discrepancies seem to appear, it is either because we may not be in possession of all the facts, or what is more likely, we fail to understand these records.

To illustrate the folly of building an argument against the historical accuracy of the Bible on what appears as alleged discrepancies, we will let a case in the Old Testament—the death of Aaron—serve our purpose.

In Numbers 20: 25-29 it says that Aaron died on Mt. Hor, while in Deuteronomy 10: 6 it says that Aaron died in Mosera. This case has often been used by the critics as conclusive proof that the Bible is not the infallible Word of God.

But what are the facts in this case?

Authorities say that the significance of Mosera is unknown, hence a contradiction cannot be said to exist between two words the exact meaning of one of which is unknown.

Moreover, it is the opinion of Prof. J. L. Porter that Mosera is the name of a general district in which Mt. Hor was situated, and Dr. Haley believes that Mosera signifies a stopping-place at the foot of Mt. Hor. If the particular spot on the top of Mt. Hor where Aaron died had no place name, would it not be inevitable that in the record the nearest place that had a name would be mentioned as the place where Aaron died? Thus it is apparent that there exists no discrepancy in these two accounts. Doubtless this case has special application to all other apparent discrepancies in the Bible including the genealogies of our Lord Jesus Christ.

In the case of the latter there are no contradictions, and the average mortal as well as the scholar need not hesitate to anchor his faith to these inspired records.

The story of the Virgin Birth, including the lineage of Jesus, is natural, reasonable and plain, and furnishes the most convincing proof of their genuineness. But, alas, how often is the Bible misconstrued in order to support a preconceived opinion or bolster up a false hypothesis?

# CHAPTER IV

## OBJECTION

**If Jesus had a miraculous human origin he would not have concealed so momentous a fact from his disciples.**

This on the surface sounds like a plausible objection, but it smacks rather of the reasoning of school-boys than of mature minds and honest seekers after the truth. It is the argument from silence which has recently been stressed by Rev. Harry Emerson Fosdick, D.D., and others in reference to John and Paul, and which will be examined in the next chapter.

### A Presumptuous Objection

As to the silence of the Lord Jesus regarding his Virgin Birth, is it not presumptive to speculate on what he should or should not have said? John is the authority for saying that his book contains only a mere fragment of what our Lord had said and done. Our Lord also assured his disciples that he had many things to say unto them but they could not hear them now, or understand or believe them.—John 16:12. To argue from our Lord's silence as to his miraculous conception is, to say the least, begging the question. There may be rare cases where this sort of argument is permissible, where all the circumstances would naturally and logically support it, but such is not the case with our Lord, for he said many things, as we shall see later, that can only be interpreted and understood in the light of his Virgin Birth. If the argument from silence is admissible, then it should work both ways. For instance, our Lord who, doubtless, was an ideal member of Joseph's household, never referred to Joseph as his father, so far as the records show, though he did refer to Mary as his mother.—John 19:26. Would it not be more reasonable to suppose that had the story of His Virgin Birth been untrue He would have denied it, as such a story would have cast serious reflection upon the good name of his mother? But after having said this, nevertheless, the argument from silence pro or con carries little weight and should seldom be admitted as evidence. There is little gained by premising assumptions of this sort. The fact of the Virgin Birth was a matter too delicate and private to be discussed openly. But this much is known, the sacred story had become current in our Lord's day. Elisabeth, the mother of John the Baptist, knew it—Luke 1:39-45.—and gradually it became the common possession of all the disciples. So stupendous and glorious a fact could not long be concealed.

### Virgin Birth Gradually Disclosed

We are now discussing a great matter in the heart of spiritual reality, a matter that is vitally related to the disclosure of the Kingdom of God and the appearance of the King, and also to the method of making his truth known. The Incarnation could not be announced by our Lord in an off-hand manner, as if he were making known a principle or law in mathematics, or were a mere reformer agitating a program of social reconstruction, or a politician submitting to men a political platform. God is never in a hurry, and he does not give a cut and dried, mechanical revelation of himself. Divine truth could only have been gradually revealed as the writers of the Bible were morally qualified to receive it. And the reception and understanding of the truth is ever conditioned on faith, humility, reverence, sincerity of heart, and obedience to the light already seen. This principle of comprehending the truth, which operates unceasingly and of necessity, was illuminated by our Lord when he said: "If any man will do God's will he shall know of the doctrine,"—John 7:17—and, "No man knoweth who the Son is but the Father; and who the Father is, but the Son, and he to whom the Son will reveal Him"—Luke 10:22.—and was interpreted by Paul: "The natural man receiveth not the things of the Spirit of God: for they are foolishness unto him; neither can he understand them because they are spiritually discerned."—1st Cor. 2:14. Our Lord in speaking of entrance into the Kingdom, revealed this same moral law: "Except a man be born again he cannot see the Kingdom of God"—John 3:3—much less enter into the Kingdom and understand it.

The disciples had to grow into the spiritual understanding of our Lord. It was, in a sense, with them as it is with us—one step at a time. The new birth is the first essential, then Kingdom truth opens up before their expanding vision. The Incarnation can be revealed to men only by the revealer of God's truth—the Holy Spirit. The carnal mind doubts it. The rationalists are living in another kingdom—the kingdom of Nature, and they cannot see or comprehend spiritual truth.

### Resurrection and the Virgin Birth

What has been stated leads, naturally, to a consideration of the relation of our Lord's resurrection to the revelation of his Incarnation. It cannot be too strongly emphasized that the larger and more perfect understanding of our Lord was impossible to his disciples until after his resurrection. Our Lord well knew that to reveal to them the fact of his supernatural conception prior to his resurrection, would have been fruitless. It was the resurrection that attested the truth of all He had said and done, and that flooded, so to speak, His whole incarnate life with the very light of God. After He had completed His redemptive work on Calvary, and had conquered sin and death, His disciples saw clearly, as they could not have seen it before, that Jesus was the Son of God. On resurrection ground they could see the Lord in the light of a divine perspective. Prior to the resurrection His mortal flesh veiled their eyes. Because the Holy Spirit is now the presiding presence in their lives they see the real Christ. His Virgin Birth, cross, resurrection, heavenly mediation, and spiritual presence in every trustful heart, as well as His future personal manifestation in glory, constituted to them the spiritual vision of Him who is now their ascended and glorified Lord. That is why it was impossible to give the written Word regarding the Christ before his victory over the grave. The resurrection is the solution of the mystery concerning our blessed Lord.

**Unity of Our Lord's Life and Work**

And this leads us to remark that, in this progressive revelation of Jesus Christ, it is clear that his life cannot be divided into sections. No one event can be separated from all the other events in His life. When men believe in the Christ of God they believe in the Christ of the Virgin Mary, as well as the Christ who died in man's stead, and who arose and lives as Saviour, Lord and coming King. The life and work of Christ are one—a divine unity—embracing his pre-existence, assumption of our humanity, his vicarious death, resurrection and everlasting triumph with his saints. Step by step, one divine act of love, one revelation after another is the way He made Himself known. His virgin Birth was the first great credential of His deity and love for men; His miracles were a cluster of the same credentials; His death was His supreme act of vicarious sacrifice for sin, when He poured out His blood for the redemption of mankind; His resurrection was the divine attestation to all he had said and done; and His personal second coming will be such a manifestation of glory and triumph as the universe has never beheld.

When men say: "I believe in the living Christ and not in the Christ, Virgin born,'' they are talking sheerest nonsense. When they say: ''Throw away your belief in the atonement, for it is Easter morning in theology,'' they simply reveal crass ignorance of the Christ of the New Testament. It required the Incarnation as well as Calvary and the resurrection to present to men a perfect revelation of God, and the true object of saving faith. The religious liberalist, with his destructive scalpel, cannot divide up in this fashion our divine Lord. When Paul wrote that our Lord ''was declared to be the Son of God with power by the resurrection from the dead''—Rom. 1:4—he did not intend to suggest, or that it might be implied that the Incarnation need not be embraced in faith, for in his other teachings he made it plain that the self-emptying was as necessary as the cross and the open grave. True Christian faith says: Because of His miraculous birth I believe that He is God; because of His death on the cross I believe that He is God; because of His resurrection I believe that He is God. All are integral parts of the one glorious self-manifestation of the Son of God in our humanity.

And care should be taken to admit of no qualifications here.

There are those who say: "I do not believe in the deity of Christ because of his Virgin Birth; I believe in his Virgin Birth because I believe in his deity." In other words, they are unwilling to affirm the Virgin Birth on the authority of the Word of God, but on the basis of a purely rationalistic process of reasoning regarding Jesus Christ. By this the basis of authority is shifted from God's infallible truth to the individual. This is Modernism in essence. But can we afford to thus think so slightingly of the testimony of Scripture as to one event in our Lord's life and yet accept the testimony of Scripture regarding other events in his life? Such an attitude is both illogical and inconsistent. If Scripture is authority for part it is for the whole of our Lord's life. The only proper and honest attitude toward this doctrine is to affirm our faith in the deity of Christ on the authority of the Word of God. I believe therefore that Jesus Christ was God because his Virgin Birth reveals it, and that on the authority of the Word of God; and I also believe in the Virgin Birth because Jesus Christ was God.

It is not a mere expression of dogmatism to say that they who deny the Virgin Birth are only mere professors of Christ, and that between all such and the true vision of the Son of God "there is a great gulf fixed," a dead line of philosophic speculation, as dark as the darkest night, as hopeless as sin and doom—the impassible barrier which men have raised by their unbelief. The true vision of Jesus Christ comprises his whole self-manifestation, and begins with his Incarnation, yet it is in the light of his resurrection that we learn the true significance of all that he was, and all that He said, and all that He had done and that makes clear the necessity of a miraculous human origin. In all this we find the secret of the silence of our Lord Jesus Christ regarding his birth from a Virgin. He knew that his victory over death would furnish the unanswerable proof of the sacred story as the writers of the Gospels relate it.

**Virgin Birth Must Be Assumed**

It is necessary here to take another step, and note that in all our Lord's teachings concerning himself the fact of his Incarnation can be seen in the background as that great event from which his human personality sprung. While He did not teach directly that He was Virgin born, nevertheless, our highest reason compels us to see underlying all His teachings, and, as the only possible key to their interpretation, the assumption of a supernatural human origin. The centuries have been baffled to account for Jesus Christ on the basis of any other hypothesis, and what faith accepts on the authority of the Word of God, reason also demands as the only possible explanation of him. Here faith, reason, Scripture, and the witness of the Holy Spirit in Christian experience, for nineteen hundred years, agree as one. In facing the fact of Christ reason must ever postulate the Incarnation, as faith ever cries: "Lord, I believe; help thou mine unbelief."—Mark 9:24.

**What Our Lord Said of Himself**

Over and over again our Lord both claimed and demonstrated that he was more than man. He could well afford to challenge men with the question, "What think ye of Christ? Whose son is he?" Did they reply that he was the son of Joseph? If not, why not? They did say that He was "the son of David," by which they intended to imply that He was not, as He had claimed to be, the son of God. Unbelief would honor Him to that extent. But our Lord comes back with the rejoinder: "How then does David in the spirit call him Lord? saying, The Lord said unto my Lord, sit thou on my right hand till I make thine enemies thy footstool. If David then called him Lord how is he his son? And no man was able to answer a word."—Matt. 22:44-46.

Take another case: In reply to the question, "Whom do men say that I the son of man am?", His disciples reported the opinions that were current regarding our Lord, and they said: "Some say that thou art John the Baptist; some Elias, and others Jeremias, or one of the prophets."—Matt. 16:13-14. Is it not significant that no one of them affirmed that he was the son of Joseph? This elimination of Joseph was not because of belief on the part of the Jews in the re-incarnation of souls, as some have supposed, in order to evade the fact of our Lord's deity. The pagan doctrine of the re-incarnation of souls never was acceptable to the Jews. The ablest minds in our Lord's day were baffled to account for him on the basis of any hypothesis, natural, philosophical, or theological, aside from the assumption of his deity. They well knew that to argue in behalf of Joseph as an explanation of Christ's unique and marvelous personality and supernatural power was utterly ridiculous. Here then was the one great problem—how to account for Jesus Christ. They could account for the historic characters in their nation, as Abraham, Moses and David, but here is One that baffled all analysis. Men have ever been unable to define, analyze or explain Deity, and when they saw God in the human form of Jesus Christ their confusion and utter perplexity was quite natural. Were Jesus Christ to appear in human form today, the greatest minds would be bewildered to account for him. It was the greatness, the superiority of Jesus Christ that, on several occasion seemed to arouse the animosity of his countrymen, especially when he affirms his divine origin—that he was greater than Abraham, that "before Abraham was, I am." Their only reply took on the form of Billingsgate and physical persecution, and they shouted "liar!" "devil!" and "took up stones to stone Him."—John 8:56-58. Calling ugly names and resorting to stones constituted a lame argument against the deity of our Lord, yet it has always been typical of those who shut their minds to the truth. We see it today in Turkey, and in Russia, and even in America, though here in our country it takes on the form of ridicule and boycott of the greatest prophets of God in the twentieth century—the "Fundamentalists"—by an ecclesiastical black hand movement to bar from the pulpits all those who are loyally standing for our Lord Jesus Christ and his truth.

### The Supreme Question

To the men of our Lord's time the great question was not whether he was born of a Virgin, but was he, as he claimed to be, "the Son of God?" If they gave assent to the latter, belief in a miraculous birth would logically follow. *Here was and is the crux of the whole matter.* The battle raged around Him because of His claim to Deity. It was for making this claim, and that He would return to earth in visible form, that He was tried before Pilate and condemned to die.—Matt. 26:63-68. And an unbelieving world is still rejecting His claim. This age-long unbelief is manifesting itself today in much of our education, secular and religious. While outwardly the attack is being made on the Virgin Birth, the underlying motive is to destroy the faith of men in the supernatural Christ.

### Claim For A Divine Sonship

Our Lord claimed for himself a unique Sonship, that he was the eternal Son of God, in contradistinction to the modern doctrine that all men are the sons of God.

This is the truth that the religious liberalists are rejecting today, and their contention constitutes a denial of the very heart of the Christian Revelation.

It is well that we take a rapid survey of this claim made by our Lord, as it is presented in the Gospels. We find that His divine Sonship was witnessed to by God, by Himself, angels, men and demons. The Angel announced it to Mary—Luke 1:32-35; the Father bore witness to it at His baptism and transfiguration.—Matt. 3:17; 17:5; the demons in men gave their testimony to it—Matt. 8:29; Peter confessed it—Matt. 16:16-18; the unbelieving Jews admitted that our Lord made such a claim—John 10:33; John the Baptist testified to it—John 1:18; 3:31; and our Lord affirmed it over and over again —Mark 14:61-62; John 3:13-16; 8:23, 35, 36, 42 and 9:35. Here is a great array of witnesses. Let us examine a few of these and learn afresh the stupendous nature of this claim and see what it involves:

Our Lord Jesus Christ submitted the question to his disciples: "Whom do men say that I the Son of man am?

"And they said, Some say that thou art John the Baptist: some Elias; and others, Jeremias, or one of the Prophets.

"He said unto them: But whom say ye that I am?

"And Simon Peter answered and said, Thou are the Christ, the Son of the living God."

In response to Peter our Lord mentions for the first time his Church. He says:

"Blessed art thou, Simon Bar-jona: for flesh and blood hath not revealed it unto thee, but my Father which is in heaven.

"And I say unto thee, That thou art Peter, and upon this rock I will build my Church; and the gates of hell shall not prevail against it."—Mat. 16:13-18.

Here then we have a remarkable prophecy and promise regarding the Church. The Church is built on a confession of the deity of our Lord. 2. The Church is a Divine Institution possessing supernatural life and power. 3. The Church was created an aggressive, militant force that can never call retreat, and to fulfil her mission, must attack evil in all its forms and pull down the gates of hell from their hinges. "The gates of hell shall not prevail against it," but must ultimately fall before the moral onslaughts of Christ and his Church. Truth must ultimately win! 4. From this it is clear that the objective of conquest for this victorious Church is the whole world. But this prophecy has been fulfilled only in part, nevertheless, e'er long the last great battle will have been fought between Christ and his Church on one hand and the anti-Christ and his world power on the other hand, and then this glorious prophecy will be fulfilled, and the Kingdom of God rule the world. But what is the great incentive, the dynamic, the battle-cry of the Church for all time? Is it not this: "Thou are the Christ the Son of the living God?" This is the faith that conquers the powers of hell and brings in the everlasting victory. "Thou art the Christ";—Thou art Deity; Thou art God.

It is significant that in the first and last recorded utterances of our Lord he reveals both his Sonship and supernatural power.

When in the temple at the age of twelve His mother affectionately chided him, saying: "Thy father and I have sought thee sorrowing"; but our Lord instantly replied: "Wist ye not that I must be about my Father's business?"—Luke 2:48-49. "My Father's business" in contradistinction to Joseph as His father. Of course Joseph was His legal father and it was in this sense in which His noble mother employed the term. But note how quickly our Lord took occasion to forestall any misleading conclusion that might result from her words. He virtually said: "My Father is not a carpenter, and my business is not the carpenter's craft. My Father is God, and I must be about my Father's business."

And note His final words:

"All power is given unto me in heaven and in earth.

"Go ye therefore and teach all nations, baptizing them in the name of the Father and of the Son and of the Holy Spirit.

"Teaching them to observe all things whatsoever I have commanded you: and, lo, I am with you alway, even unto the end of the world."—Matt. 28:18-20.

All power in the earth; all power in

the universe; all power in all worlds. Here is Omnipotence—here is God.

The Jews admitted that on one occasion they had sought to kill our Lord because he claimed "that God was his Father, thus making himself equal with God."—John 5:17-18. Our Lord does not retract one word that he had spoken to them, but rather enlarged upon it saying, "The Son can do nothing of himself, but what he seeth the Father do: for what things soever the Father doeth, *these also doeth the Son.*" The Son can do what the Father doeth. Here also is Omnipotence—here is God. Then, in what follows, he reveals to them his work as the Son of God.

The Father shows Him all that the Father doeth, i.e., He has the Knowledge of God.

The Son like the Father hath power to quicken the dead.

To the Son all judgment hath been committed.

The Son should be honored as the Father is honored.

The Son imparts everlasting life.

The Son like the Father hath life in
Himself.
The hour cometh when the Son shall
call all men out of their graves.
My works witness to all this.
The Father witnesses to all this.
The Scriptures witness to this.
—John 5:20-39.

What then is the conclusion that must be drawn from all these teachings of our Lord and from the remarkable testimonies given regarding him? Is it not that He was a supernatural Being and had a miraculous human origin?—that He was, as Matthew and Luke record, conceived of the Holy Spirit, born of a Virgin, very God of very God? We can well afford to challenge reasonable, fair-minded men to arrive at any other sane interpretation of our Lord and Saviour Jesus Christ, from the records as given of him in the Gospels.

# CHAPTER V

## OBJECTION

**If Jesus Christ had been Virgin born, John and Paul who wrote most of the New Testament would not have been silent regarding it.**

We come again to the argument from silence, if it can be so honored, for silence cannot affirm or deny. Matthew and Luke are two good witnesses, and any court would decide a case on the testimony of two reliable witnesses. Does it not appear irrational to argue against Matthew and Luke from the alleged silence of John and Paul?

But what does John say?

"In the beginning was the Word, and the Word was with God, and the Word was God."—John 1:1.

"He was in the world, and the world was made by him, and the world knew him not."—John 1:10.

"And the Word was made flesh, and dwelt among us, and we beheld his glory, the glory as of the only begotten of the Father, full of grace and truth."—John 1:14.

These passages are sufficient to reveal the attitude of John to the Virgin Birth. It is true he did not refer directly to that great event for he followed the example of our Lord, hence he assumed it in his writings.

A deadly heresy had arisen in John's day—a "denial that Jesus Christ had come in the flesh," and John wrote his Gospel to refute that heresy.

Look at his opening passage: He did not begin with the Incarnation, nor with our Lord's human descent, but with one stroke of his pen John begins to trace the divine descent of our Lord back beyond Adam, back before the morning stars sang together, before worlds were made and systems framed, back into eternity, and says: "In the beginning was the Word"—the Logos, the active Agent of Almighty God.

In his first verse John predicated three facts regarding our Lord:

1. His eternity—"In the beginning was the Word."

2. His unity with God—"And the Word was with God."

3. His Deity—"And the Word was God."

Then he proceeds to show throughout his Gospel the glory, authority and power of the eternal Son of God. The whole book assumes a miraculous birth.

We will let Dr. James Orr state the position of John as to the Incarnation. His statement comprises a list of facts that cannot be refuted.

"Do not John's words assume an exceptional mode of birth? Are they not presumptive evidence of what the other Gospel writers so plainly reveal? It would be as reasonable to argue that John's words meant to deny that Jesus was ever born at all as that he meant to deny that his birth was such as Luke and Matthew describe . . . . John had the Gospels of Matthew and Luke in his hand when he wrote his Gospel, at a time when the Virgin Birth was already a general article of belief in the Church. Doubtless John knew of the Virgin Birth. Does he repudiate it? [No.] Does he contradict it? [No.] Does he correct it? [No.] Then we have a right to believe that he accepted it. Such a story, if untrue, would have been a slur on Mary's good name, and John, who was commissioned by Jesus to care for his mother, would have resented the slander."—"The Virgin Birth of Christ."—page 107.

**Alleged Silence of Paul**

There are those who say that Paul also knew nothing of the Virgin Birth, for, they affirm, that if the great Apostle had heard the story and believed it he would not have remained silent regarding it when he wrote his epistles.

But what was true of John was likewise true of Paul. It was not Paul's purpose to discuss the first advent in a literal fashion, for he was well aware that this had been done by Matthew and Luke, and that the Christian people all knew about the Virgin Birth in his day.

Paul's purpose in writing was a varied one, but particularly to make clear the fact of the atonement, resurrection and second advent; consequently he passes over all the incidents in Christ's life, for he knew that these had been related by other writers. It would be as reasonable to argue that Paul did not believe in our Lord's miracles as to state that he placed no credence in his Virgin Birth, for he was silent as to both. Paul's great compelling themes were those just enumerated, and so his defense of the Gospel centers in them, particularly in the resurrection. He knew well that the greatest support of the Virgin Birth was found in the resurrection, therefore he built his argument on the matchless character, mediation, risen life, intercession, and spiritual presence and power of Christ, as seen in his ever-expanding and conquering Church. All these facts, in the thinking of Paul, presupposed the Incarnation. To him the resurrection was the keystone in the Christian arch, and the Incarnation, vicarious sacrifice and character of Christ were all attested by his triumph over death. These then are the proofs of the Incarnation which Paul presented and has his argument ever been successfully refuted?

**Paul Assumed the Virgin Birth**

It should be emphasized, however, that Paul in his writings did assume the fact of the Virgin Birth. Let him speak for himself:

"Who being in the form of God, thought it not robbery to be equal with God: But made himself of no reputation and took upon him the form of a servant, and was made in the likeness of men."—Phil. 2:7.

"For what the law could not do in that it was weak through the flesh, God sending his own Son in the likeness of sinful flesh, and for sin condemned sin in the flesh."—Rom. 8:3.

"But when the fulness of time was come, God sent forth his Son, made of a woman, made under the law, to redeem them that were under the law, that we might receive the adoption of sons."—Gal. 4:4-5.

In these remarkable passages Paul makes clear the purpose for which "God sent forth his Son,"—1, to redeem men from sin; 2, that we might become by faith adopted sons. Note the facts as Paul states them:

"was made in the likeness of men."

"God sending his Son in the likeness of sinful flesh, and for sin condemned sin in the flesh."

"God sent forth his Son, made of a woman, made under the law."

"To redeem them that were under the law, that we might receive the adoption of sons."

The thought running through these wonderful passages is, that "our Lord voluntarily enters our nature, yet there is a clear distinction between his deity and humanity here suggested. He is one of us yet not of us."

Paul's thought could be put in Luke's phrase, "that holy one that shall be born," because God is in His origin.

I am sure that from these passages it cannot be said that "Paul did not even distantly allude to the Virgin Birth" of the Son of God, as Dr. Harry Emerson Fosdick has asserted in a recent sermon—"Shall the Fundamentalists Win," and that he and others, who seem to deny the Virgin Birth, cannot fairly use what he terms "the silence of John and Paul" in order to disprove that great miracle.

For a fitting conclusion to this part of our discussion a quotation will be given from Dr. Sutton's pamphlet.

"There are many places where the writer of the Book of Esther might have mentioned the name of God, yet he does not mention it once, but no one concludes that he therefore knew nothing of God's existence, nor that he regarded His existence as of slight importance. The argument from silence is a dangerous weapon. Mark you, what we are asked to do is to give up belief in the Virgin Birth, not because any New Testament writer denies it but because certain New Testament writers do not affirm it clearly, though two New Testament writers do affirm it in the clearest possible way."

# CHAPTER VI

## OBJECTION

**The disciples of Jesus held two traditions regarding him—one that he was the Son of God, the other that he was the Son of Joseph; and since his disciples differed as to this matter why should men concern themselves over it.**

This objection was received by the writer from a learned New England critic.

The passages which are alleged to furnish a basis for this argument against the Virgin Birth will be examined. This is an important matter and should receive most careful attention, for, doubtless, if these passages should be misunderstood, as evidently is the case with the objector referred to above, the fact of the Virgin Birth would be weakened in the thought of some. If, however, these passages should seem to sustain the above objection, the weight of evidence would still remain on the side of the doctrine of the Virgin Birth.

But let us examine closely this alleged tradition in the light of the Scriptures which are claimed as its chief support. These passages are as follows:

> "Is not this the carpenter's son?"—Matt. 13:55.
>
> "And Jesus himself began to be about thirty years of age, being, (as was supposed), the son of Joseph."—Luke 3:23.
>
> "We have found him of whom Moses in the law and the prophets did write, Jesus of Nazareth, the son of Joseph."—John 1:45.
>
> "And they said: Is not this Jesus, the son of Joseph, whose father and mother we know."—John 6:42.

In Matt. 13:55, we simply have a quotation, giving the words spoken by the Jews, who, when they saw the wonderful works of our Lord were unable to account for him on natural grounds; therefore they said: "Is not this the carpenter's son?" It is evident that there is nothing here to show that the disciples held to any such tradition.

The reference in Luke 3:23 has been explained in chapter III. It was seen that Joseph's name was used as the legal head of his household.

Regarding John 1:45, "We have found him of whom Moses in the law and the prophets did write, Jesus of Nazareth, the son of Joseph," it should be observed that these words are a quotation from Philip, who had just decided to become a disciple of our Lord, and who up to this time had not heard of the Incarnation, hence they cannot lend support to the claim that there was held by our Lord's disciples a tradition that he was the son of Joseph. Possibly Philip's ignorance of the Virgin Birth may be accounted for from the fact that he was a Galilean. Nowhere do we learn that our Lord demanded faith in his Virgin Birth as a condition of discipleship, but he did make acceptance of him as the Son of God and Messiah from heaven a condition of discipleship, and in so doing the Virgin Birth is naturally assumed, though, as has been shown heretofore, for good and delicate reasons it could not be discussed openly by our Lord.

Indeed it is evident that Philip so viewed our Lord as the true Messiah from heaven, for this is what his words would most naturally convey—"We have found him of whom Moses in the law and the prophets did write." Of whom did the ancient prophets write but of the promised Messiah from heaven?

It is significant that Nathanael, who next enlisted as a disciple, was, as our Lord said by way of commendation, "an Israelite indeed in whom is no guile," and who, immediately, recognizing the deity of our Lord, declared: "thou art the Son of God," thus indicating that the true vision of our Lord's deity was possible to Nathanael because of the purity of his character. "The pure in heart shall see God." Nathanael was a great crystal-clear soul. May it not also be possible that in our Lord's words to Nathanael we find a rebuke of Philip's misguided idea which expressed the common notion among the unbelieving Jews that our Lord was the son of Joseph? At any rate, there is nothing here in this case to prove the claim that there existed among the disciples a tradition that our Lord was the son of Joseph.

In the next case, John 6:42, we have only a quotation. "And they said: Is not this Jesus the son of Joseph, whose father and mother we know?" These words were spoken by the Jews, who were not disciples, and were occasioned by our Lord's remarkable discourse on "the bread which came down from heaven," and that those who partake of that bread would be raised up at the last day. It was at this that the unbelieving Jews murmured, "because, as he said, I am the bread which came down from heaven, and they said, Is not this the son of Joseph?" Our Lord's reply furnishes us with a remarkable commentary, to-wit: that unbelief can never accept the fact of the Incarnation, for this truth is morally exclusive from all, except those who are the children of faith.

Surely then, judging from these passages, there is no ground for the view that there existed a tradition among the disciples that our Lord was the natural son of Joseph.

There was one condition of discipleship—acceptance of the Lord Jesus as Messiah and Son of God. So far as the records show, this condition had generally been complied with, especially so after the resurrection. Even the thief on the cross revealed by his prayer that he had seen in the dying Saviour proof of his deity, for he cried: "Lord, remember me when thou comest into thy Kingdom." Luke 23:42.

## CHAPTER VII

### OBJECTION

**The story of the Virgin Birth was suggested to Christ's disciples by the old pagan myths of the gods becoming incarnate in men, and is simply a poetic description of the greatness of Jesus.**

This is the latest invention, and probably the most subtle and treacherous advanced against the Virgin Birth of Christ, the one most calculated to deceive uninformed people, and of which much has been made by the rationalists in recent years. This theory therefore calls for examination.

Its proponents have endeavored to convince the Christian world that the powerful impression made by our Lord upon his disciples led them to worship him and accept him as the Messiah from heaven, and so they argue that the pagan myths furnished them with an illustration of our Master's greatness and mode of coming into this world. In other words, Matthew and Luke had no intention of writing up their story as fact; their object was to give a poetic description of the greatness of Jesus Christ.

One well-known critic of the Virgin Birth of Christ, Dr. Harry Emerson Fosdick, in speaking of this, says: "Pythagoras, Plato, Augustus Caesar, and others were called virgin born."

But what are the facts? The pagans believed that the gods could come to earth and become incarnate in men. Their conception as to this is, perhaps, the most base and revolting thing we find in literature, ancient or modern. A pagan god comes to a pure family and takes the wife, or daughter, the one which best suits his depravity, and the offspring is a super-man, a god-man, a hero.

So debasing are these revolting myths that in one case we find that a god, Zeus by name, tells how he had improper relations with a maiden by transforming himself into a serpent. Soltau tells that

Alexander testified that he "was begotten of a serpent that was not the bodily son of Philip." He states that the Emperor Augustus "was careful that the fable should be widely diffused to the effect that his mother was once while asleep in the Temple of Apollo visited by the god in the form of a serpent and that in the tenth month afterward he himself was born. The Emperor did everything in his power to spread the belief that the god Apollo was his father."

In these ridiculous stories there is no suggestion that Alexander's mother or Augustus' mother was a virgin. No pagan writer claimed virgin birth for any one of their heroes. They did claim that their heroes — Alexander, Caesar and others—were sons of the gods.

These are the facts regarding these pagan myths which the modern rationalists affirm served as a foundation for the chaste and beautiful story of the Virgin Birth of our divine Lord.

Of course, such stories are the merest buffoonery, and the wisest people in the pagan nations did not believe them. Who, except a politician, who sought to win the adoration of the people, would say that his father was a god in the shape of a serpent or beast or bird or lover? But such myth stories, as told by the ancients, are less absurd than the present-day claim of the rationalists, that we are all the offspring of monkeys, apes, lizards, fish and tadpoles.

**Tertullian's Testimony**

Tertullian, a minister in the early Church, who was familiar with these myths, says:

"God's own Son was born—but not so born as to make him ashamed of the name of Son, or of His paternal origin. It was not His lot to have as His father, by incest with a sister or by violation of a daughter, or another's wife, a god in the shape of a serpent . . . for his vile end, transforming himself into the gold of Danaus. These are your divinities upon whom these base deeds of Jupiter were done."—The Virgin Birth of Christ, page 169.

Tertullian was showing these pagans

that their myths were only subjects of public ridicule, and that there was no basis of comparison between their revolting fables and the Gospel records of the Virgin Birth of Christ. Nevertheless, our modern Bolshevists in religion, who are making war on the supernatural in the Bible, and who have the audacity to air their absurd nonsense, even in Christian pulpits, dare to suggest that the chaste story of the Virgin Birth of Christ is only a poetic sequel to these foul tales.

### False Claims Refuted

But our opponents reply:

"Buddha and Zoroaster and others were claimed by their followers to have been virgin born, and nearly every great religious leader is believed by his disciples to have had a supernatural birth."

It is true that adherents of these pagan religions do claim virgin birth or a supernatural origin for their leaders, but it is not true, however, that these claims were made by those who knew, personally, Buddha, Zoroaster and others. No ancient Buddhist, for example, made any such claim for him. Dr. Orr, whom we have quoted, and than whom the modern world has produced no greater authority, says: "No pagan writer of note for at least two hundred or three hundred years after Buddha's time, claimed that he was virgin born."—Virgin Birth of Christ, pages 171-172.

As we have shown heretofore, the New Testament was all written in the first century, and the story of the Virgin Birth of Christ was not something manufactured centuries after he was born, but was current and believed in his day by those who heard him and saw his wonderful works and attested by their blood the fact of his resurrection.

That the reader may feel assured that we have not misrepresented the fact as to Buddha—and what is true of Buddha is equally true of the founders of other pagan religions—we shall submit some further corroborative testimony.

In "The Message of Buddha," by Subharda Bhikkhu, and edited by I. E. Ellam who is the general secretary of the Buddhist Society of Great Britain and Ireland, this writer makes no claim for

Buddha as having been virgin born. If there had been any such tradition in any of the ancient writing concerning Buddha, doubtless this author would not have failed to refer to it.

Max Muller, who is recognized as a great authority on oriental religions, is silent regarding any such claim as having been made by ancient Buddhists.

Maurice Maeterlinck, the Belgian writer, in his book entitled: "The Great Secret," in which he treats of oriental religions, lays no claim to Buddha as having been believed by ancient Buddhists to have been virgin born.

Dr. Robert E. Speer of New York says: "The stories of the life of Buddha in the Buddhist Scriptures which resemble at all the stories in the Gospels, resemble them in the same way in which medieval legends resemble them, and moreover, they arose long after Buddha's death."—The Light of the World—Page 64.

Maeterlinck reminds his readers that the peoples of various countries "are familiar with the old myth of the child born of a virgin and that the first Jesuit missionary to China discovered that the miraculous birth of Christ had been anticipated by Huf-Ke who lived 3468 before Jesus"—page 68.

Thus it is seen that there is no historical data which can justify the claim for Buddha and others as having been virgin born, but it is entirely different with our Lord Jesus Christ. There was, as we have seen, a myth story which some authorities say probably originated in India, though no one ventures to say when or where it had its origin. It is purely an unverified myth.

In the light of all these facts, what must be our conclusion? Is it not fair to say, that in the custom of the ancients to eulogize their leaders, as Augustus Caesar and others, as having been the products of the gods, we find no basis for an argument against the Virgin Birth of Christ? Every student of history knows that there had never been found anything in the lives of those ancient leaders to convince any sane person that they had been supernaturally born, and the intelligent people of those times did not accept those stories as true.

It is, however, entirely different with

Christ. The story of His birth is chaste, refined and beautiful, and is supported by trustworthy witnesses—Matthew and Luke Mary and Elisabeth—or by what may be viewed as sound historical evidence, and conforms with the exalted spiritual character of the Bible throughout. Does not the record seem natural and altogether reasonable in the light of the character and events in our Lord's life?

### Christ and Prophecy

Moreover, another striking contrast of the greatest significance is seen in the Messianic predictions as found in the Old Testament and fulfilled in the life of Christ. Nothing like this can be said of Buddha, or Mohammed, or any founder of a pagan religion. In this fact of fulfilled prophecy we find one of the strongest proofs of the inspiration of the Bible, as a glance at history will show. The Bible predicted the dispersion of the Jews among all the peoples of the world, the extinction of their national life, and also the destruction of Assyria, Babylonia, Egypt, Greece and Rome, as it predicts the extinction of all governments at the appearance of the great King and the establishment of God's universal Kingdom of righteousness and peace. And history is simply the unfolding of God's plan for the ages, as that plan is revealed in the Bible.

In this connection, it is well to remind ourselves of two or three cf the most outstanding Messianic prophecies which were fulfilled in Christ, and which serve to illustrate his unique character and place in history.

### His Virgin Mother

"Behold a virgin shall conceive and bring forth a son, and shall call his name Immanuel."—Isa. 7:14.

### Place of His Birth Foretold

"But thou, Bethlehem, Ephratah, though thou be little among the thousands of Judah, yet out of thee shall he come forth unto me who is to be a ruler in Israel; whose goings forth hath been of old, from everlasting."—Micah 5:2.

### Sufferings and Atonement for Sin

"But he was wounded for our transgressions, he was bruised for our iniquities, the chastisement of our peace was upon him; and with his stripes we are healed.''—Isa. 53:5-12. (Read the entire chapter).

**Universal Dominion**

''For unto us a child is born, unto us a son is given, and the government shall be upon his shoulder, and his name shall be called Wonderful, Counsellor, the Mighty God, the Everlasting Father, the Prince of Peace. Of the increase of his government and peace there shall be no end. The zeal of the Lord of hosts will perform this.''—Isa. 9:6-7.

Can anything like this be said of any other founder of a religion? Surely there is no ground for comparison. Jesus Christ stands out alone and unique among all the sons of Adam, and the argument from pagan myths advanced to disprove his miraculous birth is the sheerest moonshine; it falls to the ground as does every other theory which denies the fact that he was God.

### Virgin Birth and Other Religions

But we must return for a moment to the objection, that other religions have in their sacred writings the story of a virgin birth. Granted that this is correct, yet it cannot in any way invalidate the trustworthiness of the New Testament record of our Lord's birth from a Virgin. To affirm the contrary only reveals muddled thinking. Dr. Sutton in his admirable pamphlet already referred to, says:

"Widespread belief in a Virgin Birth would rather lead us to conclude that there must be something in it, just as the fact that some kind of belief in God has been and is universal in an argument for and not against God's existence" [and just as the fact that belief in the resurrection of the body by the ancient Egyptians and others may serve to suggest that God was preparing mankind for the final authoritative revelation of this fact by our Lord Jesus Christ]. "If anyone will read the virgin birth stories of other religions, or even the accounts of our Lord's birth that are found in the Apocryphal New Testament, he will see that they are not to be mentioned in the same breath with the accounts we have in the first and third Gospels. We do not reject the Bible because other religions have sacred books; one of our reasons for accepting it is that it is so different from all other sacred books known to us. Just so we do not reject the Virgin Birth because other religions have taught birth of a virgin, but our faith in the Virgin Birth of Christ is strengthened because the accounts we have of it are so much more delicate and refined, so much more real, and on a so much higher plane than similar accounts we know."

This discussion is concluded with another quotation from Dr. Orr's famous and matchless classic—"The Virgin Birth of Christ"—a book that should be on the desk of every preacher and teacher, and in the home of every Christian. In summing up his conclusions in Chapter six—"Mythical Theories of Origin of Narratives of the Virgin Birth, Alleged Heathen Analogies,"—he says:

"The theories of mythical origin have one after another been tried and found wanting. The Jewish theories confute the Gentile; the Gentile theories confute the

Jewish; the new Babylonian theory destroys both, and itself perishes with them. The one thing that does not crumble beneath them is the historical fact'' of the Incarnation of the Son of God in our humanity.

# CHAPTER VIII

## OBJECTION

**In calling himself "the Son of man" did not Jesus Christ virtually deny the story of his Virgin Birth**

This title, "the Son of man," originated in heaven. It was the name which God gave to his great prophet Ezekiel, thus making him, in his official designation, a type of the Lord Jesus Christ in his humanity, who is the prophet of the new covenant of grace.

The prophet Isaiah also presents the Messiah as the son of man, the suffering servant of Jehovah. The Jews were offended at this conception of Messiah, hence they rebelled against what they believed to be a scandously degrading notion on the part of Isaiah. They were unable to comprehend that the Messiah would perform a sacrificial ministry. It was probably Isaiah's fifty-third chapter, in which he portrayed the nature, sufferings and atonement of the great Deliverer, that was the cause of his rejection by the Jews. And the Jewish people still have the scales on their eyes—they are blind to this sublime revelation of the great plan of God for the redemption of the world.

How beautiful and glorious is this divine title of our Lord Jesus Christ. It was to reveal its true inner significance, in both its relation to his divine nature and ministry to men, that our Lord so frequently employed the term. We hear Him ask his disciples: "Whom do men say that I the Son of man am?" When Peter gave the true reply—"Thou art the Christ the Son of the living God," our Lord at once made it clear that flesh and blood had not revealed it unto Peter, but his Father which is in heaven. And he added: "Upon this rock I will build my Church," and no power shall prevail against it. The "rock" undoubtedly was Peter's true confession of the human and divine nature of Jesus Christ, for our Lord associated both titles here as the supreme revelation of himself—"the Son of man," and "the Son of the living God." This then is His name, in which we see the human and divine blended in One. It is upon the confession of two natures in one Person—the God-man—that the Church of Christ is built, and apart from this faith there can be only a spurious Church—an apostate Christianity.

### Our Lord's Humanity

The Lord Jesus Christ was pathogenetic in his humanity, the procreation of which came from the Virgin Mary. The two human sexes are singular in nature for Eve was taken from Adam. It is unnecessary here that we go into a discussion of what some term "the scientific aspect of the Incarnation," for our Lord's birth from a Virgin cannot find much if any support in science, even though it be claimed that in some departments of nature life is propagated by one sex. The true Christian accepts the fact on the basis of the Word of God. That is sufficient for him. He believes in the inspiration and divine authority of the Bible.

The first Messianic prophecy, as given

in Genesis 3:15, states that it is the seed of the woman, and not of the man, that shall bruise the serpent's head. Thus in this prediction our Lord is seen as a human being without having a human father. He was truly human, "very man of the substance of the Virgin Mary his mother," but the union of His humanity with His God-head could not in any sense make inappropriate the designation of Himself as "the Son of man." He was indeed "bone of our bone and flesh of our flesh," and He loved to speak of Himself as "the Son of man"—the true Representative of humanity, living on man's level, "the servant of all." There was a just and holy pride in His great soul when He declared: "I am among you as he that serveth."—Luke 22:27.

Note how rich and full of profound significance is the revelation which He gives of Himself in the following words:

"For even the Son of man came not to be ministered unto but to minister and to give his life a ransom for many" or as the Greek has it, "in the place of many."—Mark 10:45.

"The Son of man must suffer many

things . . . and after that he is killed he shall rise the third day.''—Mark 9:31.

''And as they came down from the mountain he charged them that they tell no man till the Son of man were risen from the dead.''—Mark 9:9.

''And then shall they see the Son of man coming in the clouds with great power and glory.''—Mark 13:26.

These quotations show how our Lord loved to associate the title ''Son of Man'' with all the chief events in his wondrous life—with his most humble service, with his sufferings, his death on the cross, his resurrection, and his coming again in glory. He is ever ''the Son of Man.''

"A great High Priest our nature wears,
The guardian of mankind appears."

**Reason for Loving Jesus Christ**

And this is one of the principal reasons why our blessed Lord has captured the imaginations and hearts of men—why we love him. He sacrificed Himself even unto death because He loved us. He assumed the limitations of man's life because He loved us. And what did all this involve? Here He was limited in time to one generation, confined to a single tongue, heard only by those who came within range of His voice; and the Word which He was eternally with the Father is now tabernacled in flesh, not so much to reveal as to veil Omnipotence. He assumed the nature of the loveless, the sinning and lost, because of the great moral and spiritual possibilities and needs of men, and because He loved us so.

And in our human life of sorrow, suffering and sin, the trials and struggles of man arose, for the nature which He had assumed was in conflict with the good. Temptations assailed Him from every side, "yet without sin." It is little we know of the struggles beneath the calm surface of His life. How alive He became to the problems of our heart-broken world! He suffered and loved as only the purest nature, the holiest Being could suffer and love. In His ears poured the cries of broken-hearted mothers, abandoned sinners—demon-possessed men. O the glory of this suffering Servant of Jehovah! How near He has come to us, and His glory lies in that He has come so near to us.

**God Made Known**

But it was necessary that our Lord should thus become "the Son of man" in order to reveal God, for how can we conceive of the Infinite Personality being made intelligible and real to us but through a human personality. We feel this as a need on our part, and the only response to that need is found in Him who is the revelation of God to man and man to himself, i.e., as man is and as he appears in the divine Ideal of manhood. Apart from Jesus Christ—"the Son of man" and Son of God—the special revelation of God is greatly restricted. Even the work of the Holy Spirit is to reveal our blessed Lord. Jesus Christ is the center of all revelation as recorded in the Bible. The universe suggests and confirms our faith in a Supreme Intelligence, but it cannot reveal to us the heart of our Father-God. Hence God comes to man through man. "Christ emptied himself—Phil. 2:7—not of his deity, but of its form; not of the divine reality, but of its outward and glorious manifestation."

Here, in Him, we see God and may know God as our Father. Jesus Christ is the ladder Jacob saw which unites earth to heaven. In Him God and man meet on ground of pardon, everlasting friendship and peace. As our Lord said: "he that hath seen me hath seen the Father," —John 14:9—and to see God in Jesus Christ is to know God and love him. Through Jesus Christ we come face to face with the Father. "And this is life eternal, that they might know thee the only true God and Jesus Christ whom thou hast sent."—John 17:3. Therefore only He could say: "I am the way the truth and the life."—John 14:6. He is the way to life, for He is the principle of union between God and man through whom that union is realized in us. In Him we see the original type of man in all his freshness and glory. All hail! thou perfect "Son of man," and Son of God, heaven's unselfish Visitor, seeking through our eyes and hearts the race of men. We wonder not that angels announced His nativity and one of nature's luminaries escorted the shepherds to His infant abode.

**The Supreme Revelation**

The Virgin Birth of our Lord was a necessary disclosure of the wondrous revelation of God's love for the world. Love, which is an attribute of deity, was the eternal motive which moved the Son of God to become "the Son of man" in his Incarnation. His birth was a nativity of love; His words were jewels of love; His miracles were wonders of love; His death was the epitome of love; His resurrection was the logical triumph of love; and His personal reappearance and man's deliverance from the last enemy—death—will be the everlasting confirmation and eternal glory of His love.

But words are utterly impotent here; they cannot portray the life of "the Son of man"; even His works of greatest mercy reveal not the depths of his infinite heart. They are as drops to the ocean, as sparks to the sun, as grains of golden sand glistening in a tiny outflow from a mountain of richest gems. The Virgin Birth, the lowly manger, the humble service at the bench, the restless nights, the weary limbs, the human poverty, the aching heart, the dark Gethsemane, the bloody sweat, the pierced feet, the awful cross, the redeeming death all speak eloquently; yet this can only give but a glimpse of the great love of "the Son of man." At His death, that wondrous event at which the sun veiled his face, we see God's love pleading with a wayward, sorrowing world. O mighty Christ of Calvary, how wonderful! Calvary, because of what transpired there for men, became the center of the universe. There is no place like Calvary. It is better to go to Calvary than to college. Here we learn the great philosophy—the philosophy of love. Here we learn the greatest of all the sciences, the science of redemption. "Here words fail, their backs are broken, they cannot tell the story." At His lovely cross "the Son of man" and Son of God gives the true revelation of sin, righteousness and pardon. It is here that He bestows sight for blindness, purity for filth, robes for rags, love for hate, light for darkness, life for death, and the pardon, joy and peace of heaven for the guilt and sorrow and curse of sin. It was a vision of the love of "the Son of man," and Son of God that Saul of Tarsus had on the way to Damascus, and that won his life and made him lay down his weapons of warfare and do homage to Christ. It was this vision, of the love of God in Christ for sinful men, that conquered the proud Roman Empire and that shall yet conquer the world. O wondrous "Son of man" and Son of God!—very man of very man, very God of very God, perfect in His humanity, altogether glorious in His deity, the victorious Champion, Saviour and Leader of men.

> "Son of man, they crown, they crown
> Him;
> Son of God, they own, they own Him;
> With His name all heaven rings."

In the light of all the facts connected with this divine designation of Himself, as "the Son of man," surely we find an argument for rather than against the fact of His Incarnation.

The objection to Christianity by the old philosopher Celsus of the third century was, that the appeal of the Gospel of Christ was to the sinful and lost.

He says: "In our mysteries those are invited to come nigh who are of clean hands and pure speech, who are unstained by crime, who have a good conscience toward God, who have done justly and lived uprightly. The Christians say, 'Come to us, ye who are sinners, ye who are fools or children, ye who are miserable, and ye shall enter the kingdom of heaven.' Christ, say they, was sent to save sinners. Was he not sent to help those who have kept themselves from sin? They pretend that God will save the unjust man if he repents and humbles himself."

"Such indeed is," as Philip Mauro has well said: "the voice of the wisdom of this world; and the teachings of the Jewish Rabbis of Christ's day, as to sinners was practically the same." And such would be the viewpoint of the world today had not Jesus Christ come and given an entirely new revelation of God's love and salvation for men.

Celsus unwittingly has given a remarkable eulogy of Jesus Christ, as did the scribes and Pharisees in our Lord's day. They also said, with scorn and contempt,

"This man receiveth sinners and eateth with them."—Luke 15:2. Glory to His name! "For the Son of man has come to seek and to save that which was lost."—Luke 19:10.

### Recapitulation

Having submitted the argument in behalf of the Virgin Birth of our Lord, we now conclude with a recapitulation as follows:

1. It is obvious that science does not and cannot consistently deny the Virgin Birth of Christ.

2. The only two accounts we have of the earthly origin of our Lord tell us that he was begotten of the Holy Spirit and born of a Virgin.

3. These records, as given by Matthew and Luke, are admitted by all scholars of nearly every shade of opinion, to be genuine products of the Apostolic Age.

4. "These Gospels have come down to us in their integrity."—Dr. Orr.

5. The records, as given by Matthew and Luke, are complementary and independent, and show that these writers did not compare notes.

6. These records are not contradictory but corroborative of each other.

7. The writings of Mark, John and Paul do not contradict Matthews and Luke, but assume the birth of our Lord from a Virgin.

8. No other reasonable explanation can be given of the unique personality, teachings and supernatural power of Jesus Christ apart from belief in his Virgin Birth.

9. The doctrine of divine immanence cannot account for Jesus Christ.

10. No exact interpretation can be given of our Lord's teachings concerning himself apart from the fact that he was the incarnate Son of God.

11. The disciples of our Lord did not hold two traditions concerning him, one that he was the son of Joseph, the other that he was Virgin born.

12. The Virgin Birth was an article of Christian faith and believed by the Church from its beginning.

13. The Virgin Birth of our Lord is obviously a fulfilment of prophecy.

14. Many of the most eminent biblical scholars, including Harnack, admit that

the story of our Lord's earthly origin could not have originated in pagan myths.

15. The glorious doctrine of the Virgin Birth clearly implies a miracle in our Lord's human origin.

16. The significance of the Virgin Birth cannot be understood apart from the purpose for which our Lord came into the world, namely, to save sinners, to create new spiritual life in men, to establish a spiritual kingdom, and this is the work of God alone.